step-by-step
everyday cooking

THE AUSTRALIAN
Women's Weekly

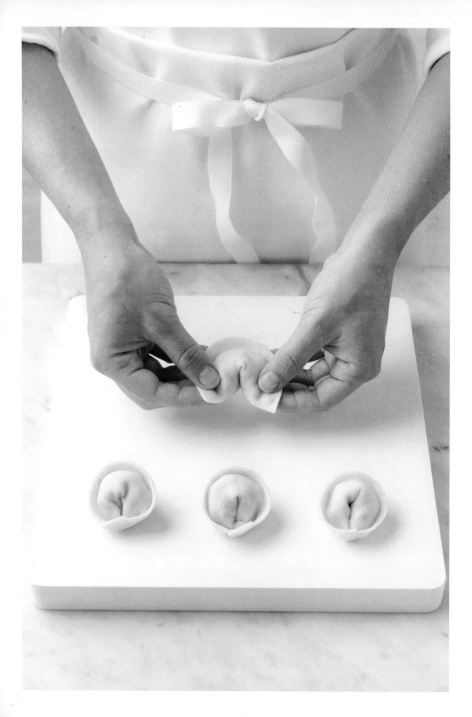

CONTENTS

AUSTRALIAN CUP AND
SPOON MEASUREMENTS
ARE METRIC.
A CONVERSION CHART
APPEARS ON PAGE 77.

We've made our best-loved recipes accessible to everyone, even beginner cooks, by adding easy step-by-step images and instructions. These classic recipes demonstrate many different cooking techniques - once you've learned them you'll be able to cook almost anything.

Pamela Clark

Food Director

HERB OMELETTE

prep + cook time **20 minutes** serves **4**
nutritional count per serving **24.4g total fat**
(8.2g saturated fat); 1254kJ (300 cal);
0.6g carbohydrate; 20.1g protein; 0.2g fibre

12 eggs
2 tablespoons each finely chopped fresh
    flat-leaf parsley, chervil and chives
1 tablespoon finely chopped fresh tarragon
⅓ cup (80ml) water
20g (¾ ounce) butter
1 tablespoon olive oil

1 Lightly whisk eggs, herbs and the water in
large bowl until just combined.
2 Heat a quarter of the butter and 1 teaspoon
of the oil in small omelette pan. When butter is
just bubbling, add a quarter of the egg mixture;
tilt pan to cover base with egg mixture. Cook
over medium heat until omelette is just set. Use
a spatula to lift and fold omelette in half; cook
further 30 seconds. Carefully slide omelette
onto serving plate.

3 Repeat with remaining butter, oil and egg
mixture (wiping out the pan after each
omelette), to make a total of four omelettes.
Serve immediately.

tips Use room temperature eggs. Overbeating eggs
will make the omelette tough. Using a mixture of
butter and oil to cook the omelette stops the butter
from burning. Using an omelette pan makes it easier
to fold and remove the omelette from the pan. Do not
wash omelette pan with soapy water, just wipe out
with a damp cloth. Washing it will make it lose its
non-stick surface.

Add a quarter of the egg mixture,
gently tilting the pan to cover the
base. This ensures even cooking
of eggs.

Using a small spatula or fork, draw
sides of eggs towards the centre of
the pan, allowing the uncooked
mixture to run underneath.

Once set, carefully flip the side of
the omelette towards the centre to
form a neat semi-circle. Remove
pan from heat and serve.

POACHED EGGS

prep + cook time **5 minutes** makes **4**
nutritional count per egg **5.3g total fat**
(1.6g saturated fat); 309kJ (74 cal);
0.2g carbohydrate; 6.7g protein; 0g fibre

2 teaspoons white vinegar
4 eggs

1 Half-fill a large shallow frying pan with water;
add vinegar. Bring to the boil.
2 Break one egg into a small bowl or cup.
Swirl the boiling water with a spoon, then slide
egg into pan. Repeat with three more eggs.
When all eggs are in pan, allow water to return
to the boil.

3 Cover pan, turn off heat; stand about
4 minutes or until a light film of egg white sets
over yolks.
4 Remove the eggs with a slotted spoon and
drain on absorbent paper. Serve eggs
immediately, with toast, if you like.

tips Fresh eggs are essential for perfect poaching.
Most store-bought eggs will have a best-before date,
however if in doubt place the egg in question in a bowl
of water. A fresh egg will lie on the bottom, while a stale
egg will float, big end up. Most poached eggs come out
of the pan with ragged edges. Once you've drained
them, place them on a cutting board and quickly trim
the edges of the whites with a small sharp knife – it's
what chefs do.

Make a whirlpool in the pan using a
wooden spoon. Putting the eggs
into the whirlpool will help keep the
whites in a neat shape.

Break one egg into a small bowl or
cup and gently slide it into the
whirlpool. Continue with remaining
eggs. Return the water to the boil.

Use a slotted spoon to remove the
eggs and drain them on absorbent
paper. At this stage you can trim
the whites if they look ragged.

CREAMY SCRAMBLED EGGS

prep + cook time **20 minutes** serves **4**
nutritional count per serving **30.2g total fat**
(16.2g saturated fat); 1375kJ (329 cal);
1.3g carbohydrate; 14g protein; 0g fibre

8 eggs
½ cup (125ml) pouring cream
2 tablespoons finely chopped fresh chives
30g (1 ounce) butter

1 Place eggs, cream and chives in medium bowl; beat lightly with fork.
2 Heat butter in large frying pan over low heat. Add egg mixture, wait a few seconds, then use a wide spatula to gently scrape the set egg mixture along the base of the pan; cook until creamy and barely set. Season to taste.
3 Serve eggs immediately, with toast, if you like.

tips For light, fluffy scrambled eggs cook them over medium heat and stir gently, yet consistently. Add chives (parsley is great too) when the eggs are a bit softer than you would like. Once cooked, be sure to remove the mixture from the pan immediately so it does not continue to cook and become dry.

Whisk the eggs, cream and chives together lightly with a fork.

Melt the butter and add the egg mixture. The heat should not be too high otherwise the eggs will become dry instead of creamy.

Fold the egg mixture from the edge of the pan to the centre. Remove from heat when eggs are still creamy and barely set.

PRAWN AND SCALLOP TORTELLINI

prep + cook time **40 minutes (+ cooling)** serves **6**
nutritional count per serving 28.6g total fat
(7.1g saturated fat); 1346kJ (323 cal);
1.8g carbohydrate; 15.3g protein; 0.2g fibre

**500g (1 pound) uncooked medium king
prawns (shrimp), shelled, deveined**
250g (8 ounces) scallops without roe
1 tablespoon olive oil
**2 tablespoons each finely chopped fresh
vietnamese mint and chervil**
**2 tablespoons finely chopped preserved
lemon rind**
220g (7 ounces) soft goat's cheese
2 teaspoons sea salt
1 teaspoon cracked black pepper
275g (9 ounces) round gow gee wrappers
lemon dressing
¼ cup (60ml) lemon juice
½ cup (125ml) olive oil
**1 tablespoon each finely chopped fresh
chervil and flat-leaf parsley**

1 Place ingredients for lemon dressing in
screw-top jar; shake well.
2 Coarsely chop prawns and scallops. Heat oil
in large frying pan; cook seafood over medium
heat until prawns change colour. Cool.
3 Combine seafood, herbs, lemon rind,
cheese, salt and pepper in medium bowl.
4 To make tortellini, place a gow gee wrapper
on bench; place 1 level tablespoon of the
seafood mixture in centre, brush edge with
water. Fold in half; bring two points together, to
make a crescent shape, press gently to seal.
Repeat with remaining wrappers and filling.
5 Cook tortellini in large saucepan of boiling
water until tortellini floats to the top; drain.
Transfer tortellini to large heatproof bowl; drizzle
with a little dressing.
6 Serve tortellini drizzled with remaining
dressing; sprinkle with extra chervil sprigs.

tips Cover gow gee wrappers with a damp tea towel to
stop them drying out while making the tortellini. The
tortellini can be made a day ahead; store tortellini, in a
single layer, covered in plastic wrap, in the refrigerator
until ready to cook. Preserved lemons are available from
delis and some supermarkets. Bear in mind that only the
rind is used in cooking, so discard the flesh from each
piece first. Rinse the rind well before chopping finely.

Place a level tablespoon of seafood
mixture in the centre of each gow
gee wrapper. Brush edges with a
little water.

Fold the wrapper in half and pinch
edge together to seal. Repeat
process for remaining wrappers
and filling.

Bring the ends of the straight edge
together to join and form a crescent
shape, pressing gently to seal.

MUSHROOM RISOTTO

prep + cook time **40 minutes** serves **4**
nutritional count per serving **15.4g total fat**
(9.4g saturated fat); 2391kJ (572 cal);
82.2g carbohydrate; 17.9g protein; 4.4g fibre

10g (½ ounce) dried chanterelle mushrooms
10g (½ ounce) dried porcini mushrooms
1 litre (4 cups) chicken or vegetable stock
2 cups (500ml) water
50g (1½ ounces) butter
100g (3 ounces) chestnut mushrooms,
   trimmed
100g (3 ounces) button mushrooms,
   sliced thickly
2 flat mushrooms (160g), halved,
   sliced thickly
4 shallots (100g), chopped finely
2 cloves garlic, crushed
2 cups (400g) arborio rice
½ cup (125ml) dry white wine
½ cup (40g) finely grated parmesan cheese
2 tablespoons finely chopped fresh chives

1 Combine chanterelle and porcini mushrooms, stock and the water in medium saucepan; bring to the boil. Reduce heat; simmer, covered.
2 Meanwhile, melt 30g (1 ounce) of the butter in large saucepan; add remaining mushrooms to pan. Cook, stirring, until mushrooms are tender and liquid evaporates; remove from pan.
3 Melt remaining butter in same pan; cook shallots and garlic, stirring, until shallots soften. Add rice; stir to coat rice in butter mixture. Return mushrooms cooked in butter to pan with wine; bring to the boil. Reduce heat; simmer, uncovered, until liquid has almost evaporated. Add 1 cup simmering stock mixture; cook, stirring, over low heat, until stock is absorbed. Continue adding stock mixture, in 1-cup batches, stirring, until absorbed between additions. Total cooking time should be about 25 minutes or until rice is tender. Stir in cheese and chives; season to taste.

tips Unlike some other rice dishes, risotto does not require you to rinse the rice before you begin to cook. In fact, the starch is essential to the dish. The initial toasting of the rice loosens the starch in each grain. As liquid is added to the rice and stirred in gently and almost constantly, more starch is released. This process will eventually leave you with a soft, creamy and evenly cooked risotto.

Using a sharp knife, cut both the flat and button mushrooms into thick slices, and trim the edges of the chestnut mushrooms.

Once the shallots and garlic are softened, stir in the rice. Cook, stirring constantly, to coat the rice with the butter mix.

Add stock, 1 cup at a time, stirring constantly and allowing each addition to be absorbed before adding the next cup.

Dip one rice paper round in a bowl of warm water for about 15 seconds until soft and pliable. Shake off any excess water.

Place a tablespoon of the prawn and noodle mixture at one end of the rice paper round. Leave a border at both ends to tuck in.

Fold the ends of the rice paper round over the filling, then roll up to enclose. Repeat the process with the remaining rice paper rounds.

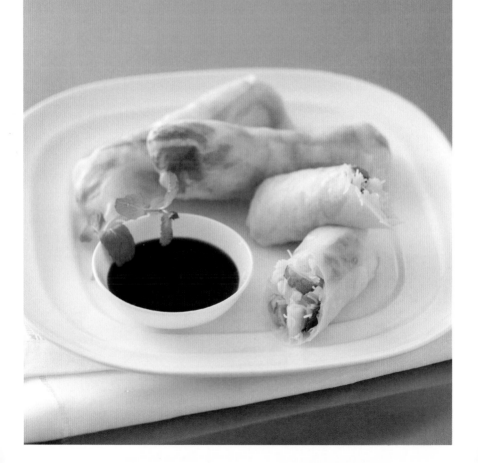

VIETNAMESE PRAWN ROLLS

prep + cook time **20 minutes** makes **12**
nutritional count per roll **0.9g total fat**
(0.1g saturated fat); 326kJ (78 cal);
10.8g carbohydrate; 5.5g protein; 1.7g fibre

50g (1½ ounces) rice vermicelli noodles,
   soaked, drained
¼ small wombok (napa cabbage) (175g),
   shredded finely
½ cup loosely packed fresh mint leaves, torn
2 teaspoons light brown sugar
2 tablespoons lime juice
500g (1 pound) cooked medium king
   prawns (shrimp)
12 x 21cm (8½-inch) rice paper rounds
hoisin dipping sauce
½ cup (125ml) hoisin sauce
2 tablespoons rice vinegar

1 Combine chopped vermicelli in medium bowl with wombok, mint, sugar and juice; season to taste.

2 Shell and devein prawns; chop meat finely.

3 Meanwhile, make hoisin dipping sauce.

4 Dip one rice paper round into bowl of warm water until soft; place on board covered with tea towel. Top with a little of the prawn meat and noodle filling. Fold and roll to enclose filling. Repeat with remaining rounds, prawn meat and noodle filling.

5 Serve rolls with hoisin dipping sauce.

hoisin dipping sauce Combine ingredients in small bowl.

tips **Soften rice paper in warm water, one at a time, for 15 to 20 seconds. Make sure you don't over-soak them as they will fall apart in your hands. The rolls can be made at the table by each diner, or ahead of time and stored in the fridge for up to 3 hours. Cover rolls with a damp clean tea towel to keep the rice paper moist.**

MINESTRONE

prep + cook time **4 hours (+ refrigeration)** serves **6**
nutritional count per serving **7.2g total fat**
(2.4g saturated fat); 865kJ (207 cal);
19.6g carbohydrate; 12.7g protein; 6.1g fibre

1 ham hock (1kg)
1 medium brown onion (150g), quartered
1 stalk celery (150g), trimmed,
   chopped coarsely
1 teaspoon black peppercorns
1 dried bay leaf
4 litres (16 cups) water
1 tablespoon olive oil
1 large carrot (180g), chopped finely
2 stalks celery (200g), trimmed, chopped
   finely, extra
3 cloves garlic, crushed
¼ cup (70g) tomato paste
2 large tomatoes (440g), chopped finely
1 small leek (200g), sliced thinly
1 cup (100g) small pasta shells
420g (13½ ounces) canned white beans,
   rinsed, drained
½ cup each coarsely chopped fresh flat-leaf
   parsley and basil
½ cup (40g) flaked parmesan cheese

1 Preheat oven to 220°C/425°F.
2 Roast ham hock and onion in baking dish, uncovered, 30 minutes.
3 Place hock and onion in large saucepan with celery, peppercorns, bay leaf and the water; bring to the boil. Reduce heat; simmer, uncovered, 2 hours.
4 Remove hock from broth. Strain broth through muslin-lined sieve or colander into large heatproof bowl; discard solids. Allow broth to cool, cover; refrigerate until cold.
5 Remove ham from hock; shred coarsely. Discard bone, fat and skin.
6 Meanwhile, heat oil in large saucepan; cook carrot and extra celery, stirring, 2 minutes. Add ham, garlic, paste and tomato; cook, stirring, 2 minutes.
7 Discard fat from surface of broth. Pour broth into a large measuring jug; add enough water to make 2 litres (8 cups). Add broth to pan; bring to the boil. Reduce heat; simmer, covered, 20 minutes.
8 Add leek, pasta and beans to pan; bring to the boil. Reduce heat; simmer, uncovered, until pasta is tender. Remove from heat; stir in herbs. Season to taste. Serve soup sprinkled with cheese.

Roast ham hock and onion in an oven for about 30 minutes or until cooked. Roasting adds a rich depth of flavour to the broth.

Remove the hock and strain the broth through a muslin-lined sieve into a large heatproof bowl. Discard the remaining solids.

Remove the ham from the hock and, using two forks, shred the meat coarsely. Discard the bone, fat and skin.

Slice through rice with a spatula to break up lumps and separate grains. At the same time, pour in the sushi vinegar gradually.

Place a nori sheet, shiny-side down, across mat 2cm (¾ inch) from the edge closest to you. Use vinegared fingers to rake rice.

Pick up mat with thumb and index fingers, holding filling in place with remaining fingers, and roll mat away from you.

BROWN RICE SUSHI

prep + cook time **1 hour 20 minutes (+ cooling)** serves **4**
nutritional count per serving **2.3g total fat**
(0.5g saturated fat); 1058kJ (253 cal);
43.1g carbohydrate; 12.8g protein; 3.4g fibre

1 cup (200g) brown short-grain rice
2 cups (500ml) water
1 tablespoon rice vinegar
3 sheets toasted seaweed (yaki-nori)
1 lebanese cucumber (130g), seeded, cut
   into matchsticks
20g (¾ ounce) snow pea sprouts, trimmed
2 tablespoons japanese soy sauce
sushi vinegar
2 tablespoons rice vinegar
2 teaspoons white (granulated) sugar
¼ teaspoon fine salt
chicken teriyaki
120g (4 ounces) chicken breast fillet,
   sliced thinly
2 tablespoons teriyaki sauce
1 clove garlic, crushed
cooking-oil spray

1 Wash rice several times in large bowl
with cold water until water is almost clear.
Drain rice in strainer for at least 30 minutes.
2 Meanwhile, make sushi vinegar and
chicken teriyaki.
3 Place rice and the water in medium
saucepan, cover tightly; bring to the boil.
Reduce heat; simmer, covered, about
30 minutes or until water is absorbed.
Remove from heat; stand, covered, 10 minutes.
4 Spread rice in a large, non-metallic,
flat-bottomed dish. Using plastic spatula,
repeatedly slice through rice at a sharp angle to
break up lumps and separate grains, gradually
pouring in sushi vinegar at the same time.

5 Continue to slice and turn the rice mixture
with one hand; fan the rice with the other hand
about 5 minutes or until it is almost cool. Cover
rice with damp cloth to stop it drying out while
making sushi.
6 Add rice vinegar to medium bowl of cold
water. Place one nori sheet, shiny-side down,
lengthways across bamboo mat about 2cm
(¾ inch) from edge of mat closest to you. Dip
fingers of one hand into bowl of vinegared
water, shake off excess; pick up a third of the
rice, place across centre of nori sheet.
7 Wet fingers again, then, working from left to
right, gently rake rice evenly over nori, leaving
2cm (¾-inch) strip on far side of nori uncovered.
Build up rice in front of uncovered strip to form
a mound to keep filling in place.
8 Place one-third of the cucumber, sprouts
and chicken in a row across centre of rice,
making sure the filling extends to both ends of
the rice.
9 Starting with edge closest to you, pick up
mat using thumb and index fingers of both
hands; use remaining fingers to hold filling in
place as you roll mat away from you. Roll
forward, pressing gently but tightly, wrapping
nori around rice and filling. Repeat process to
make a total of three rolls. Cut each roll into
four pieces. Serve with sauce, and wasabi, if
you like.
sushi vinegar Combine ingredients in small jug.
chicken teriyaki Combine chicken, sauce and
garlic in small bowl. Spray heated small frying
pan with cooking-oil spray for 1 second. Cook
chicken, stirring, until cooked through. Cool.

FRESH PASTA

prep time **40 minutes** makes **500g (1 pound)**
nutritional count per 100g **4.1g total fat**
(1.2g saturated fat); 1145kJ (274 cal);
46.2g carbohydrate; 11.2g protein; 2.4g fibre

2 cups (300g) plain (all-purpose) flour
2 teaspoons salt
3 eggs

1 Sift flour and salt onto work bench or into
large bowl; make a well in the centre.
2 Break eggs into well; using fingers,
gradually mix flour into eggs. Press mixture into
a ball. Knead dough on floured surface about
10 minutes or until smooth and elastic.

3 Cut dough in half; roll each half through
pasta machine set on thickest setting. Fold
dough in half; roll through machine again.
Repeat folding and rolling, adjusting setting on
machine to become less thick with each roll,
dusting dough with a little extra flour when
necessary. Roll until 1mm (1/16 inch) thick or until
desired thickness is reached. Cut pasta sheets
into desired pasta shape.

tips Making fresh pasta is a lot simpler than many
people think. The few ingredients needed are readily
available and inexpensive, and the process can be really
satisfying. Once you have mastered the basics, have
some fun experimenting with colours and flavours by
adding pureed vegetables to the mix.

Press the dough into a ball, roll and
stretch it on a floured surface.
Using the heel of your hand, push
the dough gently along the surface.

You might find it easier to work with
a helper, so one person can turn
the crank and the other can guide
the dough into the roller.

Attach the cutting attachment to
the hand roller. Drape the sheet of
pasta over one hand as you feed it
through the roller.

STEAK WITH PEPPER SAUCE

prep + cook time **25 minutes** serves **4**
nutritional count per serving **46.7g total fat**
(26.3g saturated fat); 2658kJ (636 cal);
5g carbohydrate; 44.2g protein; 1.4g fibre

1 tablespoon olive oil
4 x 200g (6½-ounce) scotch fillet steaks
1 stalk celery (150g), trimmed,
   chopped finely
1 medium brown onion (150g),
   chopped finely
½ cup (125ml) dry white wine
1¼ cups (310ml) pouring cream
1 tablespoon mixed peppercorns, crushed
1 tablespoon coarsely chopped fresh thyme

1 Heat half the oil in large frying pan; cook steaks, in batches, until cooked as desired. Remove from pan; cover to keep warm.
2 Heat remaining oil in same pan; cook celery and onion, stirring, until vegetables soften. Add wine; stir until liquid is reduced by half. Add cream and peppercorns; bring to the boil. Reduce heat; simmer, uncovered, stirring occasionally, about 5 minutes or until sauce thickens slightly. Remove from heat; stir in thyme. Season to taste.
3 Serve steaks drizzled with sauce and, if you like, potato chips.

tips It is fine to use just one 300ml carton of cream for this recipe. Make sure the pan is hot before adding the steaks, this helps seal in the juices. Cook presentation side of steak first, to get the correct colour. Only turn steaks once during pan-frying. Continual turning will result in dry, tough steaks. Cook the vegetables in the same pan and then add the wine which "deglazes" the pan. This picks up all the colour and flavour from cooking the steak, resulting in a rich sauce.

Place the steaks in the pan and cook for 2 minutes or until browned. Turn over and cook until done to your liking.

Pour the liquid in all at once. Scrape the brown bits on the bottom of the pan loose with a wooden spoon.

Once sauce has thickened slightly, remove pan from heat and stir in fresh thyme. Serve immediately with steak.

PORK AND VEGETABLE STIR-FRY

prep + cook time **30 minutes** serves **4**
nutritional count per serving **13.2g total fat**
(2.9g saturated fat); 1647kJ (394 cal);
30g carbohydrate; 37g protein; 2.9g fibre

2 tablespoons peanut oil
600g (1¼ pounds) pork fillets, sliced thinly
1 large brown onion (200g), sliced thinly
1 clove garlic, crushed
340g (11 ounces) asparagus, trimmed, cut
   into 4cm (1½-inch) lengths
2 medium red capsicums (bell peppers)
   (400g), sliced thinly
½ cup (125ml) plum sauce
2 tablespoons light soy sauce

1 Heat 1 tablespoon of the oil in wok; stir-fry
pork, in batches, until browned. Remove pork
from wok.
2 Heat remaining oil in wok; stir-fry onion and
garlic 1 minute. Add asparagus and capsicum;
stir-fry until softened.
3 Return pork to wok with combined sauces;
stir-fry until pork is cooked as desired.

tips Serve this stir-fry with boiled or steamed rice, if you like. Make sure you cut all your vegies into similar sized pieces – strips or bite-sized pieces work well. This ensures that they all cook at the same rate. If you cut your vegetables on the diagonal, it not only improves the appearance of the dish, it maximises their exposure to the heat. You could use chicken, beef or seafood in this recipe instead of pork. Make sure all your ingredients are prepared and immediately at hand before starting to stir-fry. Heat the wok to very hot before adding the oil, then tilt the wok to coat all over in oil. Cook food in batches so the heat of the wok does not reduce. Toss food constantly so it doesn't stick to the base of the wok. A wok chan is used to keep food moving and turning constantly. The angle and curved edge of a chan's wide, shovel-like blade are designed to fit the curve of the wok.

Add the pork in batches, to avoid overcrowding, as this reduces the wok's heating capacity, stewing the meat instead of stir-frying it.

Add vegetables according to density – the onion and garlic should be stirred in first, followed by the capsicum and asparagus.

Return the pork to the wok once the vegetables are almost cooked. This prevents the meat from overcooking.

Cook the beef chunks in batches in a flameproof dish until they're browned. If you cook too many at a time they'll stew rather than brown.

Sprinkle the flour over the softened onion and bacon mixture and stir until the flour mixture bubbles and thickens.

Gradually add stock and wine, stirring all the time, until the mixture comes to the boil and starts to thicken.

BOEUF BOURGUIGNON

prep + cook time **2 hours 45 minutes** serves **6**
nutritional count per serving **31.4g total fat**
(12.1g saturated fat); 2658kJ (636 cal);
6.6g carbohydrate; 80.3g protein; 2.8g fibre

300g (9½ ounces) baby brown onions
2 tablespoons olive oil
2kg (4 pounds) gravy beef, trimmed,
    chopped coarsely
30g (1 ounce) butter
4 rindless bacon slices (260g),
    chopped coarsely
400g (12½ ounces) button mushrooms,
    halved
2 cloves garlic, crushed
¼ cup (35g) plain (all-purpose) flour
1¼ cups (310ml) beef stock
2½ cups (625ml) dry red wine
2 dried bay leaves
2 sprigs fresh thyme
½ cup coarsely chopped fresh
    flat-leaf parsley

1 Peel onions, leaving root end intact so onion remains whole during cooking.
2 Heat oil in large flameproof dish; cook beef, in batches, until browned. Remove from dish.
3 Add butter to dish; cook onions, bacon, mushrooms and garlic, stirring, until onions are browned lightly.
4 Sprinkle flour over onion mixture; cook, stirring, until flour mixture thickens and bubbles. Gradually add stock and wine; stir over heat until mixture boils and thickens. Return beef and any juices to dish, add bay leaves and thyme; bring to the boil. Reduce heat; simmer, covered, about 2 hours or until beef is tender, stirring every 30 minutes.
5 Remove from heat; discard bay leaves. Stir in parsley; season to taste.

QUICHE LORRAINE

prep + cook time **1 hour 30 minutes (+ refrigeration)**
serves **6**
nutritional count per serving **51.8g total fat
(35.4g saturated fat); 3139kJ (751 cal);
35.4g carbohydrate; 22.1g protein; 2g fibre**

1 medium brown onion (150g),
   chopped finely
3 rindless bacon slices (195g),
   chopped finely
3 eggs
1¼ cups (310ml) pouring cream
½ cup (125ml) milk
¾ cup (120g) coarsely grated gruyère cheese
pastry
1¾ cups (260g) plain (all-purpose) flour
150g (4½ ounces) cold butter,
   chopped coarsely
1 egg yolk
2 teaspoons lemon juice
⅓ cup (80ml) iced water, approximately

1 Make pastry.
2 Preheat oven to 200°C/400°F.
3 Roll pastry between sheets of baking paper large enough to line a deep 23cm (9-inch) loose-based flan tin. Lift pastry into tin; gently press pastry around side. Trim edge, place tin on oven tray. Cover pastry with baking paper; fill with dried beans or rice. Bake 10 minutes; remove paper and beans. Bake pastry a further 10 minutes or until golden brown; cool.
4 Reduce oven to 180°C/350°F.
5 Cook onion and bacon in heated oiled small frying pan until onion is soft; drain on absorbent paper, cool. Sprinkle bacon mixture over pastry case.
6 Whisk eggs in medium bowl; whisk in cream, milk and cheese, season.
7 Pour egg mixture into pastry case. Bake about 35 minutes or until filling is set. Stand 5 minutes before removing from tin.
pastry Sift flour into bowl; rub in butter. Add egg yolk, juice and enough water to make ingredients cling together. Knead gently on lightly floured surface until smooth; cover, refrigerate 30 minutes.

tip It's fine to use just one 300ml carton of cream.

Use the rolling pin to gently lift the pastry dough into the flan tin. Press the pastry into the sides of the tin and trim the edges.

Place a sheet of baking paper in the tin and sprinkle in some dried beans to weigh it down and keep the pastry from rising.

Once the pastry case is cooked and cooled, sprinkle cooled bacon mixture over it and pour over the custard mix.

BUTTER CHICKEN

prep + cook time **1 hour 40 minutes (+ refrigeration)**
serves **4**
nutritional count per serving **74g total fat**
(33.3g saturated fat); 4138kJ (990 cal);
20.8g carbohydrate; 59.3g protein; 6.5g fibre

1 cup (150g) unsalted raw cashews
2 teaspoons each garam masala and
    ground coriander
½ teaspoon chilli powder
3 cloves garlic, chopped coarsely
4cm (1½-inch) piece fresh ginger (20g), grated
2 tablespoons white vinegar
⅓ cup (95g) tomato paste
½ cup (140g) yogurt
1kg (2 pounds) chicken thigh fillets, halved
80g (2½ ounces) butter
1 large brown onion (200g), chopped finely
1 cinnamon stick
4 cardamom pods, bruised
1 teaspoon hot paprika
400g (12½ ounces) canned tomato puree
¾ cup (180ml) chicken stock
¾ cup (180ml) pouring cream

1 Dry-fry nuts in small frying pan, stirring, until nearly brown. Add garam masala, coriander and chilli, continue stirring, until nuts are browned lightly.
2 Blend or process nut mixture with garlic, ginger, vinegar, paste and half the yogurt until mixture forms a paste. Transfer to large bowl, stir in remaining yogurt and chicken. Cover; refrigerate 3 hours or overnight.
3 Melt butter in large saucepan; cook onion, cinnamon and cardamom, stirring, until onion is browned lightly. Add chicken mixture; cook, stirring, 10 minutes.
4 Stir in paprika, puree and stock; simmer, uncovered, 45 minutes, stirring occasionally.
5 Discard cinnamon and cardamom. Add cream; simmer, uncovered, 5 minutes. Season to taste.

tips Serve with steamed rice and warmed naan if you like. For a great pie filling add 2 large cooked potatoes, chopped, and 100g (3 ounces) baby spinach leaves to the butter chicken. Spoon the filling into a deep pie dish and top with a sheet of puff pastry. Brush with beaten egg, snip two air holes in the top and bake in a hot oven for 25 minutes or until the pastry is golden.

Cardamom pods must be bruised (crushing with the side of a knife is the easiest way) to release their fragrance and warm subtle taste.

Stir cashews in pan until almost brown. Watch constantly – a moment's inattention now and the nuts will burn.

Blend or process the spiced nuts with ginger, garlic, vinegar, tomato paste and yogurt until smooth. Transfer the paste to a large bowl.

SINGAPORE CHILLI CRAB

prep + cook time **30 minutes** serves **4**
nutritional count per serving **10.1g total fat**
(1.8g saturated fat); 723kJ (173 cal);
8.2g carbohydrate; 11.6g protein; 1.6g fibre

4 x 325g (10½-ounce) uncooked blue
   swimmer crabs
2 tablespoons peanut oil
3 cloves garlic, chopped finely
4cm (1½-inch) piece fresh ginger (20g), grated
1 fresh small red thai (serrano) chilli,
   sliced thinly
⅓ cup (85ml) bottled tomato pasta sauce
2 tablespoons chilli sauce
2 tablespoons japanese soy sauce
⅓ cup (80ml) water
2 teaspoons white (granulated) sugar
½ cup firmly packed fresh coriander
   (cilantro) leaves

1 Lift flap under body of each crab; turn crab over, hold body with one hand while pulling off top part of shell with the other. Discard shell and gills on either side of body. Rinse crab under cold water; chop body into quarters.
2 Heat oil in wok; stir-fry garlic, ginger and chilli until fragrant. Add sauces, the water and sugar; stir-fry 2 minutes.
3 Add crab; cook, covered, over medium heat, about 10 minutes or until crab has changed colour. Serve sprinkled with coriander.

tip Have finger bowls filled with warm water and lemon slices on-hand with this dish, and plenty of large napkins.

Lift the tail flap, then, with a peeling motion, pull off the top shell.

Remove and discard the whitish gills (these are known as dead men's fingers), plus the liver and brain matter.

Rinse the crab well then chop into quarters.

CHICKEN SCHNITZEL

prep + cook time **30 minutes** serves **4**
nutritional count per serving **41.5g total fat**
(9g saturated fat); 3097kJ (741 cal);
35.4g carbohydrate; 55.7g protein; 2.3g fibre

4 chicken breast fillets (800g)
¼ cup (35g) plain (all-purpose) flour
2 eggs
1 tablespoon milk
2½ cups (175g) stale white breadcrumbs
2 teaspoons finely grated lemon rind
2 tablespoons each finely chopped fresh
    flat-leaf parsley and basil
⅓ cup (25g) finely grated parmesan cheese
vegetable oil, for shallow-frying

1 Using meat mallet, gently pound chicken, one piece at a time, between sheets of plastic wrap until 5mm (¼ inch) thick; cut each piece in half.

2 Whisk flour, eggs and milk in shallow bowl, season; combine breadcrumbs, rind, herbs and cheese in another shallow bowl. Coat chicken pieces, one at a time, in egg mixture then breadcrumb mixture.

3 Heat oil in large frying pan; shallow-fry chicken, in batches, until cooked. Drain on absorbent paper.

4 Serve chicken schnitzel with lemon wedges, if you like.

tip The breadcrumb mixture lends itself to the addition of extra flavours, such as chopped thyme or rosemary, chilli or mustard powder.

Dip the pounded out chicken fillets in a batter made from flour, eggs and milk.

Put the breadcrumb mixture in a shallow dish and coat the chicken fillets on both sides.

Heat enough oil to coat the bottom of the pan and shallow-fry the schnitzels, turning once, until golden brown and cooked through.

CLASSIC FISH AND CHIPS

prep + cook time **50 minutes** serves **4**
nutritional count per serving **14.6g total fat**
(3.1g saturated fat); 2261kJ (541 cal);
55.1g carbohydrate; 39.6g protein; 4.8g fibre

1 cup (150g) self-raising flour
1 cup (250ml) dry ale
1 tablespoon sea salt
1kg (2 pounds) potatoes, peeled
peanut oil, for deep-frying
4 x 150g (4½-ounce) blue-eye fillets,
    halved lengthways

1 Sift flour into medium bowl; whisk in beer
and salt until smooth.
2 Cut potatoes lengthways into 1cm (½-inch)
slices; cut each slice lengthways into 1cm
(½-inch) chips; pat dry with absorbent paper.

3 Heat oil in large saucepan. Cook chips, in
three batches, about 2 minutes or until tender
but not brown. Drain on absorbent paper.
4 Dip fish in batter; drain off excess. Deep-fry
fish, in batches, until cooked. Drain on
absorbent paper.
5 Deep-fry chips, in three batches, until crisp
and golden brown; drain on absorbent paper.
Serve fish and chips with tartare sauce and
lemon wedges.

tip This dish is traditionally served with tartare sauce.
To make your own, combine ⅔ cup whole-egg
mayonnaise, ½ finely chopped small brown onion,
2 tablespoons finely chopped cornichons, 1 tablespoon
finely chopped drained and rinsed capers, 1 tablespoon
finely chopped fresh flat-leaf parsley and 1 tablespoon
lemon juice in a medium bowl.

Add beer to the flour and salt and
whisk together until it becomes a
smooth batter.

Dip the fish fillets into the batter
and shake off the excess.

Deep-fry the fish in batches until
golden and cooked through. Drain
the fillets well on absorbent paper.

ROAST CHICKEN WITH HERB STUFFING

prep + cook time **2 hours 15 minutes** serves **4**
nutritional count per serving **35.9g total fat**
(14.4g saturated fat); 2437kJ (583 cal);
19.4g carbohydrate; 45g protein; 1.9g fibre

1.5kg (3-pound) chicken
15g (½ ounce) butter, melted
herb stuffing
1½ cups (105g) stale breadcrumbs
1 stalk celery (150g), trimmed,
  chopped finely
1 small white onion (80g), chopped finely
2 teaspoons finely chopped fresh sage
1 tablespoon finely chopped fresh
  flat-leaf parsley
1 egg, beaten lightly
30g (1 ounce) butter, melted

1 Preheat oven to 200°C/400°F.
2 Make herb stuffing.
3 Remove and discard any fat from cavity of chicken. Rinse chicken under cold water; pat dry inside and out with absorbent paper. Fill cavity of chicken with stuffing, fold over skin to enclose stuffing; secure with toothpicks. Tie legs together with kitchen string.

4 Place chicken on oiled rack in large baking dish. Half-fill dish with water – it should not touch the chicken. Brush chicken with butter, season; roast 15 minutes.
5 Reduce oven to 180°C/350°F. Roast further 1½ hours or until chicken is cooked through, basting occasionally with pan juices. Stand 10 minutes before breaking or cutting into serving-sized pieces.
herb stuffing Combine ingredients in medium bowl; season to taste.

tips Drying the chicken thoroughly results in a crisper skin. Tying the chicken's legs together helps it to keep its shape during roasting. Placing the chicken on a rack prevents it from sticking to the pan and causing the skin to tear. The water in the baking dish creates steam, keeping the chicken moist. Basting the chicken during baking helps the skin to brown and keeps the chicken moist. A thermometer is an easy way to check whether the chicken (and stuffing) has been cooked through. A temperature of 75°C/165°F will ensure the chicken flesh will be white and its juices run clear.

Seal in the stuffing by stitching two to three wooden toothpicks through the edges of the opening, like a needle in a tapestry.

Truss the chicken with kitchen string. Hold one end of the string in each hand, loop the centre around the legs and secure in a knot.

Spoon pan juices all over chicken as it cooks in the oven. Occasional basting adds great flavour and browns the chicken evenly.

GLAZED BAKED HAM

prep + cook time **1 hour 20 minutes** serves **16**
nutritional count per serving **19.4g total fat**
(7.1g saturated fat); 2111kJ (505 cal);
22.9g carbohydrate; 59g protein; 0g fibre

½ cup (180g) honey
½ cup (125ml) maple syrup
½ cup (110g) firmly packed light brown sugar
2¼ cups (560ml) water
7kg (14-pound) cooked leg ham

1 Preheat oven to 180°C/350°F.
2 Combine honey, syrup, sugar and ¼ cup of
the water in small saucepan; stir over heat until
sugar dissolves. Bring to the boil; remove from
heat, cool 10 minutes.

3 Cut through rind of ham 10cm (4 inches)
from the shank end of the leg. To remove rind,
run thumb around edge of rind just under skin.
Start pulling rind from widest edge of ham,
continue to pull rind carefully away from the fat
up to the shank end. Remove rind completely.
Score across the fat at about 3cm (1¼-inch)
intervals, cutting through the surface of the fat
(not the meat) in a diamond pattern.
4 Pour the remaining water into large baking
dish; place ham on oiled wire rack over dish.
Brush ham all over with honey glaze. Roast,
uncovered, about 1 hour or until browned,
brushing frequently with glaze during cooking.

tip Reserve the rind from the ham after it has been
removed. When storing the ham (or the leftovers),
re-cover the leg's cut surface with the reserved rind –
this will keep it moist.

Use a small sharp knife to cut
through the rind. Gently lift it off in
one piece by running your thumb
around edge of rind.

Score the fat, about 1cm (½ inch)
deep and 3cm (1¼ inches) apart in
a diamond pattern, taking care not
to cut into the meat.

Pour water into a large baking
dish to keep the ham moist
during cooking. Brush frequently
with glaze.

Brush oil all over the roast and season with pepper. Add the roast, fat-side down, and brown. Turn the roast, cooking until browned all over.

Transfer the beef juices left in the baking dish to a small saucepan. Add brandy and bring to the boil.

Once you have added the stock, pour in the blended cornflour and water, and continue cooking until the mixture boils and thickens.

STANDING RIB ROAST
WITH ROAST VEGETABLES

prep + cook time **1 hour 50 minutes** serves **4**
nutritional count per serving **29.2g total fat**
(8.5g saturated fat); 3114kJ (745 cal);
41.1g carbohydrate; 60.4g protein; 5.4g fibre

1.2kg (2½-pound) beef standing rib roast
¼ cup (60ml) olive oil
2 teaspoons cracked black pepper
500g (1 pound) potatoes, chopped coarsely
500g (1 pound) pumpkin, chopped coarsely
500g (1 pound) kumara (orange sweet
      potatoes), chopped coarsely
½ cup (125ml) brandy
1½ cups (375ml) beef stock
1 tablespoon cornflour (cornstarch)
¼ cup (60ml) water
1 tablespoon finely chopped fresh chives

1 Preheat oven to 200°C/400°F.
2 Brush beef with 1 tablespoon of the oil; sprinkle with pepper. Heat 1 tablespoon of the oil in large shallow flameproof baking dish; cook beef, uncovered, over high heat until browned all over. Roast, uncovered, in oven about 45 minutes or until cooked as desired.
3 Meanwhile, heat remaining oil in another large flameproof baking dish; cook potatoes, stirring, over high heat until browned lightly. Add pumpkin and kumara, place dish in oven with beef; roast, uncovered, about 35 minutes or until vegetables are browned.
4 Place beef on vegetables, cover; return to oven to keep warm. Drain juices from beef baking dish into medium saucepan, add brandy; bring to the boil. Add stock and blended cornflour and water; cook, stirring, until sauce boils and thickens slightly. Stir in chives, season to taste; pour into medium heatproof jug.
5 Serve beef and vegetables with sauce.

tip **A standing rib roast is also known as a bone-in rib roast.**

ROAST TURKEY
WITH FORCEMEAT STUFFING

prep + cook time **3 hours 45 minutes**
(+ cooling & standing) serves **8**
nutritional count per serving **54.7g total fat**
(21g saturated fat); 3641kJ (871 cal);
12.8g carbohydrate; 79.6g protein; 1.4g fibre

4.5kg (9-pound) turkey
1 cup (250ml) water
80g (2½ ounces) butter, melted
¼ cup (35g) plain (all-purpose) flour
3 cups (750ml) chicken stock
½ cup (125ml) dry white wine
forcemeat stuffing
40g (1½ ounces) butter
3 medium brown onions (450g),
   chopped finely
2 rindless bacon slices (130g),
   chopped coarsely
1 cup (70g) stale breadcrumbs
½ cup coarsely chopped fresh
   flat-leaf parsley
250g (8 ounces) minced (ground) pork
250g (8 ounces) minced (ground) chicken

1 Preheat oven to 180°C/350°F. Make
forcemeat stuffing.
2 Discard neck from turkey. Rinse turkey under
cold water; pat dry inside and out with
absorbent paper. Fill neck cavity loosely with
stuffing; secure skin over opening with small
skewers. Fill large cavity loosely with stuffing;
tie legs together with kitchen string.

3 Place turkey on oiled wire rack in large
shallow baking dish; pour the water into dish.
Brush turkey all over with half the butter,
season; cover turkey tightly with two layers of
greased foil. Roast 2 hours. Uncover turkey;
brush with remaining butter. Roast, uncovered,
about 1 hour or until cooked through. Remove
turkey from dish, cover loosely with foil; stand
20 minutes.
4 Pour juice from dish into large jug; skim
1 tablespoon of fat from juice, return fat to
same dish. Skim and discard fat from
remaining juice; reserve juice. Add flour to dish;
cook, stirring, until mixture bubbles and is
well-browned. Gradually stir in stock, wine
and reserved juice; cook, stirring, until gravy
boils and thickens. Strain gravy into jug; serve
with turkey.
forcemeat stuffing Melt butter in medium
frying pan; cook onion and bacon, stirring, over
low heat until onion is soft. Cool. Combine
onion mixture and remaining ingredients in
large bowl; season.

tip To test if the turkey is cooked, insert a skewer
sideways into the thickest part of the thigh, then remove
and press flesh to release the juices. If the juice runs
clear, the turkey is cooked. Alternatively, insert a meat
thermometer into the thickest part of the thigh, without
touching the bone; the turkey is cooked when the
thermometer reaches 90°C/194°F.

Fill the large cavity until it is loosely stuffed. Make sure you don't over-stuff the cavity as the stuffing needs room to expand.

Pull the skin over the stuffing and secure with skewers. Tie the legs together with kitchen string.

After the turkey has been cooking for 2 hours, remove it from the oven, uncover and baste with the remaining melted butter.

Sprinkle the combined rosemary and sweet paprika all over the lamb. You can rub some of the mixture into the slits, if you like.

To check whether the lamb is done, insert a meat thermometer into the centre of the thickest part of the meat, away from bone and fat.

Slowly add the stock and wine, and stir over a high heat until the gravy starts to boil and thicken. Strain the gravy into a heatproof jug.

ROAST LAMB

prep + cook time **1 hour 30 minutes** serves **6**
nutritional count per serving **17.9g total fat**
(6.6g saturated fat); 2086kJ (499 cal);
32.3g carbohydrate; 47.7g protein; 5g fibre

2kg (4-pound) leg of lamb
3 sprigs fresh rosemary, chopped coarsely
½ teaspoon sweet paprika
1kg (2 pounds) potatoes, chopped coarsely
500g (1 pound) pumpkin, chopped coarsely
3 small brown onions (240g), halved
2 tablespoons olive oil
2 tablespoons plain (all-purpose) flour
1 cup (250ml) chicken stock
¼ cup (60ml) dry red wine

1 Preheat oven to 200°C/400°F.
2 Place lamb in oiled large baking dish; using
sharp knife, score skin at 2cm (¾-inch)
intervals, sprinkle with rosemary and paprika,
season. Roast lamb 15 minutes.

3 Reduce oven to 180°C/350°F; roast lamb
about 45 minutes or until cooked as desired.
4 Meanwhile, place potatoes, pumpkin and
onions, in single layer, in large shallow baking
dish; drizzle with oil. Roast for last 45 minutes
of lamb cooking time.
5 Remove lamb and vegetables from oven;
strain pan juices from lamb into medium jug.
Cover lamb and vegetables to keep warm.
Return ¼ cup of the pan juices to baking dish,
stir in flour; stir over heat about 5 minutes or
until mixture bubbles and browns. Gradually
add stock and wine; stir over high heat until
gravy boils and thickens. Strain gravy into
medium heatproof jug.
6 Slice lamb; serve with roasted vegetables
and gravy.

ROAST LOIN OF PORK WITH APPLE SAUCE

prep + cook time **2 hours (+ standing)** serves **8**
nutritional count per serving **72g total fat**
(24.1g saturated fat); 3762kJ (900 cal);
7.7g carbohydrate; 56.7g protein; 1.1g fibre

2.5kg (5-pound) boneless loin of pork, rind on
2 sprigs fresh rosemary
1 tablespoon olive oil
1 tablespoon coarse cooking salt (kosher salt)
apple sauce
3 large apples (600g)
½ cup (125ml) water
1 teaspoon white (granulated) sugar
pinch ground cinnamon

1 Preheat oven to 250°C/480°F.
2 Score pork rind with sharp knife. Tie pork at 2cm (¾-inch) intervals with kitchen string; tuck rosemary under string. Place pork in large baking dish; rub with oil, then salt. Roast about 40 minutes or until rind blisters. Drain excess fat from dish.

3 Reduce oven to 180°C/350°F. Roast pork about 1 hour. Transfer pork to plate; cover loosely with foil, stand 15 minutes before slicing.
4 Meanwhile, make apple sauce.
5 Serve pork with apple sauce.
apple sauce Peel and core apples; slice thickly. Place apples and the water in medium saucepan; simmer, uncovered, about 10 minutes or until apple is soft. Remove pan from heat; stir in sugar and cinnamon. Blend or process mixture until almost smooth.

tips As always when buying meat, your best bet is a supplier you can trust. In general, pork should have fine-grained, pale pink flesh, white fat and thin, smooth skin. Avoid any that has waxy fat or is wet, meaning it has been badly handled and may be from an animal in poor condition. Ask your butcher to roll and tie the pork at 2cm (¾-inch) intervals for you, and to score the rind, if it isn't already done.

Place pork loin on a cutting board and score the rind at 1cm (½-inch) intervals, using a sharp knife.

Place pork in a shallow baking dish and, using your fingers, rub the oil all over the skin. Rub the salt over the skin, working it into the slits.

When pork is cooked, remove from the oven and cover loosely with foil. Allow the pork to rest for about 15 minutes before cutting into slices.

STRAWBERRY CONSERVE

prep + cook time **1 hour 10 minutes (+ cooling)**
makes **1.5 litres (6 cups)**
nutritional count per tablespoon **0g total fat**
(0g saturated fat); 280kJ (67 cal);
15.9g carbohydrate; 0.4g protein; 0.5g fibre

1.5kg strawberries, hulled
1.1kg (5 cups) white (granulated) sugar
1 cup (250ml) lemon juice

1 Gently heat berries in large saucepan, covered, for 5 minutes to extract juice. Transfer berries with slotted spoon to large bowl; reserve.

2 Add sugar and lemon juice to strawberry juice in pan; stir over heat, without boiling, until sugar dissolves. Bring to the boil; boil, uncovered, without stirring, 20 minutes. Return reserved berries to pan; simmer, uncovered, without stirring, 25 minutes or until jam jells when tested.
3 Pour hot jam into hot sterilised jars; seal immediately.

tips You will need about 3 medium lemons (420g) to get the amount of juice needed for this recipe. To sterilise, place jar and lid in the dishwasher on the hottest rinse cycle. Don't use detergent. Alternatively, lay the jar and lid in a large pan, cover completely with cold water and gradually bring to the boil; boil for 20 minutes.

Add lemon juice to the sugar and strawberry juice in the pan. The lemon adds pectin to help the jam set.

Put a spoonful of jam onto a freezer-chilled saucer. Push the jam with your finger; if it wrinkles, the jam is set.

Pour the hot jam into hot sterilised jars, taking the mixture right up to the top. Seal the jars while the jam is still hot.

BASIC SCONES

prep + cook time **45 minutes** makes **35**
nutritional count per scone **2g total fat**
(1.2g saturated fat); 339kJ (81 cal);
13.2g carbohydrate; 2.1g protein; 0.7g fibre

4 cups (600g) self-raising flour
2 tablespoons icing (confectioners') sugar
60g (2 ounces) butter, chopped
1½ cups (375ml) milk
¾ cup (180ml) water, approximately
¼ cup milk, extra

1 Preheat oven to 220°C/425°F. Grease
20cm x 30cm (8-inch x 12-inch) rectangular pan.
2 Sift flour and sugar into large bowl; rub in
butter with fingertips.

3 Make a well in centre of flour mixture; add
milk and almost all the water. Use knife to "cut"
the milk and water through the flour mixture,
mixing to a soft, sticky dough. Knead dough
on floured surface until smooth.
4 Press dough out to 2cm (¾-inch) thickness.
Dip 4.5cm (1¾-inch) round cutter in flour; cut
as many rounds as you can from piece of
dough. Place scones, side by side, just
touching, in pan.
5 Gently knead scraps of dough together;
repeat pressing and cutting of dough, place in
same pan. Brush tops with a little extra milk.
6 Bake scones about 15 minutes or until just
browned and sound hollow when tapped
firmly on the top with fingers. Serve with jam
and cream.

Rub the butter into the sifted flour
and icing sugar mixture, using
your fingertips.

Add the milk and water to the bowl
and, using a flat-bladed knife, slice
through the flour mixture, mixing
until the dough is soft and sticky.

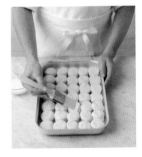

Brush the tops of the scones with
the extra milk. The scones should
be arranged so they are sitting side
by side in the pan and just touching.

Sprinkle plain flour onto the boiled pudding cloth and spread it out to cover about 40cm (16 inches).

Gather pudding cloth evenly around pudding, avoiding deep pleats, then pat the mixture into a round shape.

Suspend pudding by placing spoon over rungs of an upturned stool. Ensure there are no hanging pieces of string or cloth touching it.

BOILED CHRISTMAS PUDDING

prep + cook time **6 hours 30 minutes**
(+ standing & cooling) serves **16**
nutritional count per serving **15.5g total fat**
(9.1g saturated fat); 2090kJ (500 cal);
79.7g carbohydrate; 7g protein; 3.3g fibre

1½ cups (250g) raisins
1½ cups (240g) sultanas
1 cup (150g) dried currants
¾ cup (120g) mixed peel
1 teaspoon finely grated lemon rind
2 tablespoons lemon juice
2 tablespoons brandy
250g (8 ounces) butter, softened
2 cups (440g) firmly packed light brown sugar
5 eggs
1¼ cups (185g) plain (all-purpose) flour
½ teaspoon ground nutmeg
½ teaspoon mixed spice
4 cups (280g) stale breadcrumbs
pudding cloth (see tips)

1 Combine fruit, rind, juice and brandy in large bowl. Cover tightly with plastic wrap; store in a cool, dark place overnight or up to a week, stirring every day.
2 Beat butter and sugar in large bowl with electric mixer until combined. Beat in eggs, one at a time. Add butter mixture to fruit mixture then add sifted dry ingredients and breadcrumbs; mix well.
3 Fill large boiler three-quarters full of hot water, cover; bring to the boil. Have ready 2.5m (2½ yards) of kitchen string and an extra ½ cup of plain (all-purpose) flour. Wearing thick rubber gloves, dip pudding cloth in boiling water; boil 1 minute then remove and carefully squeeze excess water from cloth. Working quickly, spread hot cloth on bench, rub flour into centre of cloth to cover an area about 40cm (16 inches) in diameter, leaving flour a little thicker in centre of cloth where "skin" on the pudding needs to be thickest.

4 Place pudding mixture in centre of cloth. Gather cloth evenly around mixture, avoiding any deep pleats; then pat into round shape. Tie cloth tightly with string as close to mixture as possible. Pull ends of cloth tightly to ensure pudding is as round and firm as possible. Knot the corners of the cloth together to make a loop, so pudding is easier to remove from water.
5 Lower pudding into boiling water; tie free ends of string to handles of boiler to suspend pudding. Cover with tight-fitting lid; boil for 6 hours, replenishing water as necessary to maintain level.
6 Untie pudding from handles; place wooden spoon through knotted calico loop to lift pudding from water. Do not put pudding on bench; suspend by, for example, placing spoon over rungs of an upturned stool. Ensure there are no hanging pieces of string or cloth touching the pudding as it dries. If pudding has been cooked correctly, cloth will dry in patches within a few minutes; hang 10 minutes.
7 Place pudding on board; cut string, carefully peel back cloth. Turn pudding onto a plate then carefully peel cloth away completely; stand at least 20 minutes or until skin darkens and pudding becomes firm.

tips You'll need a 60cm (24-inch) square of unbleached calico for the pudding cloth. If the calico hasn't been used before, start with an 80cm (16-inch) square of calico, soak in cold water overnight. Next day, boil it for 20 minutes, rinse in cold water and cut to a 60cm square. To store pudding, remove cloth, then allow pudding to come to room temperature, wrap it in plastic wrap and seal tightly in a freezer bag or airtight container. Pudding can be stored in refrigerator up to two months or frozen up to 12 months. To reheat, thaw frozen pudding three days in refrigerator; remove from fridge 12 hours before reheating. To reheat in microwave oven, cover whole pudding with plastic wrap; microwave on medium (55%) about 15 minutes or until hot.

FEATHERLIGHT SPONGE CAKE

prep + cook time **40 minutes** serves **10**
nutritional count per serving **13.3g total fat**
(8g saturated fat); 1195kJ (286 cal);
37.2g carbohydrate; 3.8g protein; 0.7g fibre

4 eggs
¾ cup (165g) caster (superfine) sugar
⅔ cup (100g) wheaten cornflour (cornstarch)
¼ cup (30g) custard powder
1 teaspoon cream of tartar
½ teaspoon bicarbonate of soda
(baking soda)
⅓ cup (110g) apricot jam
1¼ cups (310ml) thickened (heavy) cream,
whipped

1 Preheat oven to 180°C/350°F. Grease and flour two deep 22cm (9-inch) round cake pans.
2 Beat eggs and sugar in small bowl with electric mixer until thick, creamy and sugar is dissolved. Transfer mixture to large bowl; fold in triple-sifted dry ingredients. Divide mixture evenly between pans.
3 Bake sponges about 20 minutes. Turn, top-side up, onto baking-paper-covered wire rack to cool.
4 Sandwich sponges with jam and cream. Sprinkle with a little sifted icing (confectioners') sugar, if you like.

tips Cake pans are best greased evenly with melted butter. Beating the eggs and sugar can take up to 10 minutes to get the correct volume. Using a narrow-topped bowl will allow the beaters to give volume to the egg and sugar mixture. Fold the flour into the cake mixture in a gentle, light circular motion for a lighter texture. Store unfilled sponges, wrapped well, in the freezer for up to 2 months. It is fine to use just one 300ml carton of cream for this recipe.

Sifting three times produces a lighter, finer textured cake. Hold the sifter up high to incorporate as much air as possible into the flour.

Beat the eggs and caster sugar together until the sugar is dissolved and the mixture is thick and creamy.

Use a metal spoon, a knife, or a plastic or rubber spatula to fold in triple-sifted dry ingredients.

BASIC BUTTERCAKE

prep + cook time **1 hour 30 minutes** serves **12**
nutritional count per serving **18.6g total fat**
(11.6g saturated fat); 1522kJ (364 cal);
43.5g carbohydrate; 5.1g protein; 1.1g fibre

250g (8 ounces) butter, softened
1 teaspoon vanilla extract
1¼ cups (275g) caster (superfine) sugar
3 eggs
2¼ cups (335g) self-raising flour
¾ cup (180ml) milk

1 Preheat oven to 180°C/350°F. Grease
deep 20cm (8-inch) square or 22cm (9-inch)
round cake pan; line base and side(s) with
baking paper.
2 Beat butter, extract and sugar in medium
bowl with electric mixer until light and fluffy.
Beat in eggs, one at a time. Stir in sifted flour
and milk, in two batches.

3 Spread mixture into pan; bake about 1 hour.
Stand cake 5 minutes; turn, top-side up, onto
wire rack to cool.

tips When beating in eggs, ensure each egg is
combined well in butter mixture before adding the next
egg. Do this quickly to avoid curdling. Store buttercake
at room temperature, in an airtight container for 2 days,
or freeze for up to 2 months.

Beat the softened butter, vanilla
extract and caster sugar until fluffy
and light in colour. Scrape sides of
bowl with a spatula occasionally.

Add the eggs, one at a time, with
the mixer on low speed and beat
for several seconds between each
addition. Do not overbeat.

Stir in half the flour and half the
milk. Add the remaining flour and
milk, gently stir. Beat with wooden
spoon briefly to remove lumps.

JAM ROLL

prep + cook time **30 minutes** serves **10**
nutritional count per serving **1.9g total fat**
(0.6g saturated fat); 819kJ (196 cal);
40.5g carbohydrate; 3.3g protein; 0.6g fibre

3 eggs, separated
½ cup (110g) caster (superfine) sugar
2 tablespoons hot milk
¾ cup (110g) self-raising flour
¼ cup (55g) caster (superfine) sugar, extra
½ cup (160g) jam, warmed

1 Preheat oven to 200°C/400°F. Grease
25cm x 30cm (10-inch x 12-inch) swiss roll
pan; line base with baking paper, extending
paper 5cm (2 inches) over short sides.
2 Beat egg whites in small bowl with electric
mixer until soft peaks form; add sugar,
1 tablespoon at a time, beating until dissolved
between additions. With motor operating, add
egg yolks, one at a time, beating until mixture is
pale and thick; this will take about 10 minutes.

3 Pour hot milk down side of bowl; add
triple-sifted flour. Working quickly, use plastic
spatula to fold milk and flour through egg
mixture. Pour mixture into pan, gently spreading
into corners.
4 Bake cake about 8 minutes.
5 Meanwhile, place a piece of baking paper
cut the same size as pan on board or bench;
sprinkle evenly with extra sugar.
6 Turn cake immediately onto sugared paper;
peel away lining paper. Use serrated knife to
trim crisp edges from all sides of cake.
7 Using paper as a guide, gently roll warm
cake loosely from one of the short sides. Unroll;
spread evenly with jam. Re-roll cake from same
short side. Cool.

Gently peel away the lining paper,
using a spatula to press down on
the paper. The weight of the spatula
will prevent the cake from breaking.

Using a serrated knife, trim away
the crisp edges from all sides of
the cake.

With no filling, using the sugared
baking paper as a guide, gently roll
the warm cake loosely. Once you've
spread it with jam, it will roll easily.

BASIC BUTTER COOKIES

prep + cook time **30 minutes (+ refrigeration)** makes **50**
nutritional count per cookie **4g total fat**
(2.6g saturated fat); 314kJ (75 cal);
8.6g carbohydrate; 0.9g protein; 0.3g fibre

250g (8 ounces) butter, softened
1 cup (160g) icing (confectioners') sugar
2½ cups (375g) plain (all-purpose) flour

1 Beat butter and sifted sugar in small
bowl with electric mixer until light and fluffy.
Transfer mixture to large bowl; stir in flour, in
two batches.
2 Knead dough on lightly floured surface until
smooth. Divide dough in half; roll each half into
a 25cm (10-inch) log. Wrap in plastic wrap;
refrigerate about 1 hour or until firm.
3 Preheat oven to 180°C/350°F. Grease oven
trays; line with baking paper.
4 Cut logs into 1cm (½-inch) slices; place
slices on trays about 2cm (¾ inch) apart.
5 Bake cookies about 10 minutes or until
browned lightly. Transfer cookies onto wire rack
to cool.

variations

chocolate and hazelnut Beat 2 tablespoons
sifted cocoa powder into butter and sugar
mixture, then stir in ⅓ cup ground hazelnuts
and ¼ cup finely chopped milk choc bits before
adding the flour.
dried cranberry Stir in ⅔ cup finely chopped
dried cranberries into butter and sugar mixture.
vanilla Beat 1 teaspoon vanilla extract into
butter and sugar mixture.
lemon Beat 1 teaspoon finely grated lemon
rind into butter and sugar mixture.
orange Beat 1 teaspoon finely grated orange
rind into butter and sugar mixture.

tips Cookies should feel soft in the oven even though
they're cooked. Check the cookies a few minutes before
the end of baking time – if they feel a little soft, but firm,
give one cookie a gentle push with the side of your
thumb. A cooked cookie will slide easily on the tray. The
cookies will become crisp on cooling. Store cookies in
an airtight container for up to 1 week. Keep this dough,
rolled into a log shape and tightly sealed in plastic wrap,
in your fridge for up to 3 days or in your freezer for up to
3 months. Thaw in refrigerator before cutting into slices.

Transfer mixture to a large bowl.
Stir in sifted flour, in two batches, to
take the effort out of mixing.

The dough must stay cold. Run
warm hands under cold water,
then dry before kneading quickly
and lightly.

Divide the dough in half and roll
each half into a 25cm (10-inch) log.
Refrigerate until firm.

CHOCOLATE SOUFFLE

prep + cook time **35 minutes** serves **4**
nutritional count per serving **27.1g total fat**
(16.1g saturated fat); 2040kJ (488 cal);
52.3g carbohydrate; 8.1g protein; 0.7g fibre

⅓ cup (75g) caster (superfine) sugar
50g (1½ ounces) butter
1 tablespoon plain (all-purpose) flour
200g (6½ ounces) dark eating (semi-sweet)
   chocolate, melted
2 eggs, separated
2 egg whites
1 tablespoon cocoa powder

1 Preheat oven to 180°C/350°F. Grease four
¾-cup (180ml) soufflé dishes. Sprinkle inside
of dishes with a little of the sugar; shake away
excess. Place dishes on oven tray.
2 Melt butter in small saucepan, add flour;
cook, stirring, about 2 minutes or until mixture
thickens and bubbles. Remove from heat;
stir in chocolate and egg yolks. Transfer to
large bowl.

3 Beat all egg whites in small bowl with electric
mixer until soft peaks form. Gradually add
remaining sugar, beating until sugar dissolves.
Fold egg white mixture into chocolate mixture,
in two batches.
4 Divide soufflé mixture among dishes; bake
15 minutes. Serve immediately, dusted with
cocoa powder.

tips Egg whites are vital to a soufflé's success. They
must be folded very carefully into the mixture. Use a
wide-topped bowl so folding is easier for you. Use a
whisk, spatula or large metal spoon for the folding – the
choice is yours. Some cooks like to fold a small amount
of the egg white (about a quarter) through the flavoured,
more solid mixture first to "let the mixture down" a little.
Fold in the remaining egg whites, in one or two batches
depending on the quantity. Experiment a little to
determine what works best for you and your soufflés.

Grease four soufflé dishes, then
sprinkle the insides with caster
sugar, shaking away excess. Place
the dishes on an oven tray.

Melt butter in a saucepan, then add
flour, cook for 2 minutes. Remove
from heat, add chocolate, stirring,
add egg yolks. Stir well to combine.

Transfer chocolate mixture to a
large mixing bowl. Fold in the egg
white mixture, in two batches.

CREME BRULEE

prep + cook time **55 minutes (+ refrigeration)** serves **6**
nutritional count per serving **52.1g total fat
(32.3g saturated fat); 2358kJ (564 cal);
19.8g carbohydrate; 5.8g protein; 8g fibre**

**1 vanilla bean
3 cups (750ml) thickened (heavy) cream
6 egg yolks
¼ cup (55g) caster (superfine) sugar
¼ cup (40g) pure icing (confectioners') sugar**

1 Preheat oven to 180°C/350°F. Grease six
½-cup (125ml) ovenproof dishes.
2 Split vanilla bean in half lengthways; scrape
seeds into medium heatproof bowl. Place
pod in small saucepan with cream; heat
without boiling.
3 Add egg yolks and caster sugar to seeds in
bowl; gradually whisk in hot cream mixture.
Place bowl over medium saucepan of
simmering water; stir over heat about
10 minutes or until custard mixture thickens
slightly and coats the back of a spoon.
Discard pod.

4 Place dishes in large baking dish; divide
custard among dishes. Add enough boiling
water to baking dish to come halfway up sides
of ovenproof dishes.
5 Bake custards, uncovered, about 20 minutes
or until set. Remove custards from dish; cool.
Cover; refrigerate overnight.
6 Preheat grill (broiler). Place custards in
shallow flameproof dish filled with ice cubes;
sprinkle custards evenly with sifted icing sugar.
Using finger, spread sugar over the surface of
each custard, pressing in gently; place under
grill until the tops caramelise.

tips For many, the best part about crème brûlée is the
crisp toffee on top. This is also the hardest part to get
right if you don't have a blowtorch (favoured by chefs).
But we've found topping the custards with pure icing
sugar makes it easier to caramelise them under the grill
at home. Make sure you place the crème brûlées as
close as possible to a hot grill. Surrounding the custards
with ice keeps them cool as you heat the top. Of course,
you can use a blowtorch if you have one. The adjustable
flame melts the sugar quickly, so the filling remains cool.
Professional cooks' blowtorches are available from
specialty kitchen shops.

Split the vanilla bean in half
lengthways and scrape the seeds
out with a knife.

Place the bowl over a saucepan of
simmering water. Stir the cream
mixture for about 10 minutes or
until it coats the back of a spoon.

Caramelise the sugar under a
preheated hot grill. If you have a
blowtorch, use that.

LEMON MERINGUE PIE

prep + cook time **1 hour 10 minutes (+ refrigeration)**
serves **10**
nutritional count per serving **18.9g total fat**
(11.6g saturated fat); 1772kJ (424 cal);
57.7g carbohydrate; 5g protein; 0.9g fibre

½ cup (75g) cornflour (cornstarch)
1 cup (220g) caster (superfine) sugar
½ cup (125ml) lemon juice
1¼ cups (310ml) water
2 teaspoons finely grated lemon rind
60g (2 ounces) unsalted butter, chopped
3 eggs, separated
½ cup (110g) caster (superfine) sugar, extra
pastry
1½ cups (225g) plain (all-purpose) flour
1 tablespoon icing (confectioners') sugar
140g (4½ ounces) cold butter, chopped
1 egg yolk
2 tablespoons cold water

1 Make pastry.
2 Grease 24cm (9½-inch) round loose-based
fluted flan tin. Roll pastry between sheets of
baking paper until large enough to line tin.
Ease pastry into tin, press into base and side;
trim edge. Cover; refrigerate 30 minutes.

3 Preheat oven to 240°C/475°F.
4 Place tin on oven tray. Line pastry case with
baking paper; fill with dried beans or rice. Bake
15 minutes; remove paper and beans carefully
from pie shell. Bake about 10 minutes; cool pie
shell, turn oven off.
5 Meanwhile, combine cornflour and sugar in
medium saucepan; gradually stir in juice and
the water until smooth. Cook, stirring, over high
heat, until mixture boils and thickens. Reduce
heat; simmer, stirring, 1 minute. Remove from
heat; stir in rind, butter and egg yolks. Cool
10 minutes.
6 Spread filling into pie shell. Cover; refrigerate
2 hours.
7 Preheat oven to 240°C/475°F.
8 Beat egg whites in small bowl with electric
mixer until soft peaks form; gradually add extra
sugar, beating until sugar dissolves.
9 Roughen surface of filling with fork before
spreading with meringue mixture. Bake about
2 minutes or until browned lightly.
pastry Process flour, icing sugar and butter
until crumbly. Add egg yolk and the water;
process until ingredients come together. Knead
dough on floured surface until smooth. Cover;
refrigerate 30 minutes.

Use a rolling pin to gently ease the
pastry into the flan tin, being careful
not to stretch it.

Spread the lemon filling evenly
into the cooked and cooled
pie shell. A spatula is the best
implement to use for this.

Roughen the surface of the lemon
filling before you spread the
meringue on top.

CREME CARAMEL

prep + cook time **1 hour (+ refrigeration)** serves **8**
nutritional count per serving **22.3g total fat
(13.3g saturated fat); 1526kJ (365 cal);
33.8g carbohydrate; 7.5g protein; 0g fibre**

**¾ cup (165g) caster (superfine) sugar
½ cup (125ml) water
6 eggs
1 teaspoon vanilla extract
⅓ cup (75g) caster (superfine) sugar, extra
1¼ cups (310ml) pouring cream
1¾ cups (430ml) milk**

1 Preheat oven to 160°C/325°F.
2 Combine sugar and the water in medium heavy-based saucepan; stir over heat, without boiling, until sugar dissolves. Bring to the boil; boil, uncovered, without stirring, until mixture is a deep caramel colour. Remove from heat; allow bubbles to subside. Pour toffee into deep 20cm (8-inch) round cake pan.
3 Whisk eggs, extract and extra sugar in large bowl.
4 Combine cream and milk in medium saucepan; bring to the boil. Whisking constantly, pour hot milk mixture into egg mixture. Strain mixture into cake pan.

5 Place pan in baking dish; add enough boiling water to come halfway up side of pan. Bake, in oven, about 40 minutes or until set. Remove custard from baking dish, cover; refrigerate overnight.
6 Gently ease crème caramel from side of pan; invert onto deep-sided serving plate.

tips Use a heavy pan to make the toffee. Once the sugar has been dissolved and the mixture starts to boil, watch it carefully. As soon as it starts to brown, tilt the pan until the brown areas merge. Keep tilting and turning the pan until the toffee is a rich golden colour. Remove the pan from the heat, let the bubbles subside, then pour toffee over the base of the cake pan. There is no need to coat the side of the pan, or even grease it. An aluminium cake pan gives the best results for even baking of the custard. Refrigerating the crème caramel overnight breaks down and liquifies the toffee which will make it easier to turn the crème caramel out of the pan. When you're ready to serve, use your fingers to ease the custard away from the side of the pan, gently wriggle the pan and you'll "feel" the custard floating on the caramel. Put the serving plate on top of the cake pan and quickly invert. It is fine to use just one 300ml carton of cream for this recipe.

All the sugar needs to be dissolved when you're making caramel. Brush any extra sugar from side of the pan using a dampened pastry brush.

When the caramel is a deep, rich brown, pour it into the base of a deep 20cm (8-inch) cake pan.

Put the custard into a baking dish and pour enough boiling water around the cake pan to come halfway up its side.

TARTE TATIN

prep + cook time **1 hour 30 minutes (+ refrigeration)**
serves **8**
nutritional count per serving **21.1g total fat
(13.7g saturated fat); 1860kJ (445 cal);
59.5g carbohydrate; 2.7g protein; 2.9g fibre**

**100g (3 ounces) unsalted butter, chopped
6 large apples (1.2kg), peeled,
    cored, quartered
1 cup (220g) firmly packed light brown sugar
2 tablespoons lemon juice**
pastry
**1 cup (150g) plain (all-purpose) flour
2 tablespoons caster (superfine) sugar
80g (2 ½ ounces) cold unsalted butter,
    chopped
2 tablespoons sour cream**

1 Melt butter in large heavy-based frying pan;
add apples, sprinkle evenly with sugar and
juice. Cook, uncovered, over low heat, about
40 minutes, turning apples as they caramelise.
2 Meanwhile, make pastry.
3 Preheat oven to 200°C/400°F.

4 Place apples, rounded-sides down, in
22cm (9-inch) pie dish, packing tightly to
ensure there are no gaps; drizzle with
1 tablespoon of the caramel in pan.
Reserve remaining caramel.
5 Roll pastry between sheets of baking paper
until large enough to cover apples. Peel away
one sheet of baking paper; cut pastry to fit
dish. Remove remaining paper. Place pastry
carefully over hot apples; tuck pastry around
apples.
6 Bake tarte tatin about 30 minutes or until
pastry is browned. Carefully turn onto serving
plate, apple-side up; drizzle apple with
reheated reserved caramel.
pastry Process flour, sugar, butter and sour
cream until ingredients just come together.
Knead on floured surface until smooth. Cover;
refrigerate 30 minutes.

tip **Golden delicious apples are the best apples to use,
granny smith the second best.**

Place the caramelised apples,
rounded-side down, in the pie dish.
Remember to arrange the apples in
a decorative pattern.

Cut the pastry round to fit snugly
into the pie dish and place it over
the hot apples.

Tuck the pastry carefully and evenly
down the sides of the dish – this
will form the pastry base when the
pie is inverted.

BAY LEAVES aromatic leaves from the bay tree; available fresh or dried; adds a strong, slightly peppery flavour.

BEANS, WHITE a generic term we use for canned or dried cannellini, haricot, navy or great northern beans belonging to the same family, phaseolus vulgaris.

BEEF

gravy boneless stewing beef from shin; slow-cooked, imbues stocks, soups and casseroles with a gelatine richness. Cut crossways, with bone in, is osso buco.

scotch fillet cut from the muscle running behind the shoulder along the spine. Also known as cube roll, cuts include standing rib roast and rib-eye.

standing rib roast see scotch fillet.

BICARBONATE OF SODA also known as baking soda.

BLUE-EYE also called deep sea trevalla or trevally and blue-eye cod; thick, moist white-fleshed fish.

BREADCRUMBS

packaged prepared fine-textured but crunchy white breadcrumbs; good for coating foods that are to be fried.

stale crumbs made by grating, blending or processing 1- or 2-day-old bread.

CAPERS the grey-green buds of a warm climate (usually Mediterranean) shrub, sold either dried and salted or pickled in a vinegar brine; tiny young ones, called baby capers, are also available both in brine or dried in salt. Their pungent taste adds piquancy to a tapenade, sauces and condiments.

CAPSICUM also called pepper or bell pepper. Discard seeds and membranes before use.

CARDAMOM a spice native to India and used extensively in its cuisine; can be purchased in pod, seed or ground form. Has a distinctive aromatic, sweetly rich flavour and is one of the world's most expensive spices.

CHEESE

goat's made from goat's milk, has an earthy, strong taste. Available in soft, crumbly and firm textures, in various shapes and sizes, and sometimes rolled in ash or herbs.

gruyère a hard-rind Swiss cheese with small holes and a nutty flavour. A popular cheese for soufflés.

parmesan also called parmigiano; is a hard, grainy cow's milk cheese originating in the Parma region of Italy. The curd for this cheese is salted in brine for a month, then aged for up to 2 years in humid conditions. Reggiano is the best parmesan, aged for a minimum 2 years and made only in the Italian region of Emilia-Romagna.

CHOCOLATE

Choc Bits also called chocolate chips or chocolate morsels; available in milk, white and dark chocolate. Made of cocoa liquor, cocoa butter, sugar and an emulsifier, these hold their shape in baking and are ideal for decorating.

dark eating also known as semi-sweet or luxury chocolate; made of a high percentage of cocoa liquor and cocoa butter, and little added sugar. Unless stated otherwise, we use dark eating chocolate in this book as it's ideal for use in desserts and cakes.

Melts small discs of compounded milk, white or dark chocolate ideal for melting and moulding.

CINNAMON available both in the piece (sticks or quills) and ground; one of the world's most common spices, used universally as a sweet, fragrant flavouring in sweet and savoury foods.

COCOA POWDER also known as unsweetened cocoa; cocoa beans (cacao seeds) that have been fermented, roasted, shelled, ground into powder then cleared of most of the fat content.

CORNFLOUR also known as cornstarch. Available made from corn or wheat (wheaten cornflour, gluten-free, gives a lighter texture in cakes); used as a thickening agent in cooking.

CORNICHON French for gherkin, a very small variety of cucumber. Pickled, they are a traditional accompaniment to pâté, and are also served with fondue or raclette.

CREAM

pouring also known as pure cream. It has no additives and contains a minimum fat content of 35 per cent. If a recipe here calls for an unspecified cream, this is the one we use.

sour cream a thick, commercially-cultured sour cream with a minimum fat content of 35 per cent.

thickened a whipping cream that contains a thickener. It has a minimum fat content of 35 per cent.

CREAM OF TARTAR the acid ingredient in baking powder; added to confectionery mixtures to help prevent sugar from crystallising. Keeps frostings creamy; improves volume when beating egg whites.

GLOSSARY

CUSTARD POWDER instant mixture used to make pouring custard; similar to North American instant pudding mixes.

FLOUR

cornflour see cornflour.

plain also called all-purpose; unbleached wheat flour is the best for baking: the gluten content ensures a strong dough, which produces a light result.

self-raising all-purpose plain or wholemeal flour with baking powder and salt added; make it yourself in the proportion of 1 cup flour to 2 teaspoons baking powder.

GARAM MASALA literally meaning blended spices in its northern Indian place of origin; based on varying proportions of cardamom, cinnamon, cloves, coriander, fennel and cumin, roasted and ground together. Black pepper and chilli can be added for a hotter version.

GOW GEE WRAPPERS see wonton wrappers.

HERBS

chervil also called cicily; mildly fennel-flavoured member of the parsley family with curly dark-green leaves. Available fresh and dried but, like all herbs, is best used fresh; like coriander and parsley, its delicate flavour diminishes the longer it's cooked.

chives related to the onion and leek; has a subtle onion flavour.

coriander also called cilantro, pak chee or chinese parsley; bright-green-leafed herb having both pungent aroma and taste. Used as an ingredient in a wide variety of cuisines. Often stirred into or sprinkled over a dish just before serving. Both the stems and roots of coriander are used in Thai cooking. Coriander seeds are dried and sold either whole or ground, and neither form tastes remotely like the fresh leaf.

marjoram closely related to and similar in flavour to oregano, but milder and sweeter.

mint the most commonly used variety of mint is spearmint; it has pointed, bright-green leaves and a fresh flavour.

oregano a herb, also known as wild marjoram; has a woody stalk and clumps of tiny, dark-green leaves. Has a pungent, peppery flavour.

rosemary pungent herb with long, thin pointy leaves; use large and small sprigs, and the leaves are usually chopped finely.

sage narrow, grey-green leaves; slightly bitter with a musty mint aroma.

tarragon french tarragon, with its subtle aniseed flavour, complements chicken, eggs and veal, and is perfect in a béarnaise sauce. It is also one of the herbs that make up the French *fines herbs*. Russian and mexican tarragons are slightly coarser in taste.

thyme a basic herb of French cuisine is widely used in Mediterranean countries to flavour meats and sauces.

KUMARA the Polynesian name of an orange-fleshed sweet potato often confused with yam.

LAMB

leg cut from the hindquarter; can be boned, butterflied, rolled and tied, or cut into dice.

MACADAMIAS native to Australia; fairly large, slightly soft, buttery rich nut. Store in fridge to prevent their high oil content turning them rancid.

MAPLE-FLAVOURED SYRUP is made from sugar cane and is also known as golden or pancake syrup. It is not a substitute for pure maple syrup.

MAYONNAISE, WHOLE-EGG commercial mayonnaise of high quality made with whole eggs. Must be refrigerated once opened.

MILK we use full-cream homogenised milk unless otherwise specified.

MIXED DRIED FRUIT a combination of sultanas, raisins, currants, mixed peel and cherries.

MIXED SPICE A classic spice mixture generally containing caraway, allspice, coriander, cumin, nutmeg and ginger, although cinnamon and other spices can be added. It is used with fruit and in cakes.

MUSHROOMS

button small, cultivated white mushrooms with a mild flavour. When a recipe in this book calls for an unspecified type of mushroom, use button.

chanterelle also called girolles or pfifferling; a trumpet-shaped wild mushroom, ranging in colour from yellow to orange. It has a delicate flavour and a chewy texture. Also available dried.

chestnut are cultivated mushrooms with a firm texture and strong flavour. They are available only irregularly.

dried porcini the richest-flavoured mushrooms, also known as cèpes. Expensive, but because they're so strongly flavoured, only a small amount is required.

flat large, flat mushrooms with a rich earthy flavour, ideal for filling and barbecuing. They are sometimes misnamed field mushrooms which are wild mushrooms.

NOODLES

rice vermicelli also called sen mee, mei fun or bee hoon. Used throughout Asia in spring rolls and cold salads; similar to bean threads, only longer and made with rice flour instead of mung bean starch.

NORI a type of dried seaweed used in Japanese cooking as a flavouring, garnish or for sushi. Sold in thin sheets, plain or toasted (yaki-nori).

OIL

cooking oil spray we use a cholesterol-free cooking spray made from canola oil.

peanut pressed from ground peanuts; the most commonly used oil in Asian cooking because of its high smoke point (capacity to handle high heat without burning).

PAPRIKA Ground dried sweet red capsicum (bell pepper); there are many grades and types available, including sweet, hot, mild and smoked.

PLUM SAUCE a thick, sweet and sour dipping sauce made from plums, vinegar, sugar, chillies and spices.

POLENTA also called cornmeal; a flour-like cereal made of dried corn (maize). Also the dish made from it.

PORK

fillet skinless, boneless eye-fillet cut from the loin.

ham hock the shank of the leg, which does not form part of the ham but is salted and smoked in the same way.

loin from pork middle.

minced ground lean pork.

PRESERVED LEMON whole or quartered salted lemons preserved in olive oil and lemon juice and occasionally clove, cinnamon and coriander. A North African specialty, added to casseroles and tagines to impart a rich, salty-sour acidic flavour; also added to dressings or yogurt. Available from delis and specialty food shops. Use the rind only and rinse well under cold water before using.

RICE, ARBORIO small, round grain rice well-suited to absorb a large amount of liquid; the high level of starch makes it especially suitable for risottos for its classic creaminess.

SCOTCH FILLET see beef.

SHALLOTS also called french shallots, golden shallots or eschalots. Small and elongated, with a brown-skin, they grow in tight clusters similar to garlic.

SOUR CREAM see cream.

SPONGE FINGER BISCUITS also called savoiardi, savoy biscuits or lady's fingers, they are Italian-style crisp fingers made from sponge cake mixture.

SUGAR we use coarse, granulated table sugar (crystal sugar), unless specified.

icing also known as confectioners' sugar or powdered sugar.

light brown also known as brown, a soft, finely granulated sugar retaining molasses for its characteristic colour and flavour.

TERIYAKI a homemade or commercially bottled sauce usually made from soy sauce, mirin, sugar, ginger and other spices; it imparts a distinctive glaze when brushed on grilled meat.

TOMATOES

bottled pasta sauce a prepared sauce; a blend of tomatoes, herbs and spices.

canned whole peeled tomatoes in natural juices; available crushed, chopped or diced. Use undrained.

egg also called plum or roma, these are small and oval-shaped.

paste triple-concentrated tomato puree used to flavour soups, stews and sauces.

puree canned pureed tomatoes (not tomato paste); substitute with fresh peeled and pureed tomatoes.

VANILLA

bean dried, long, thin pod from a tropical golden orchid; the tiny black seeds inside the bean are used to impart a luscious vanilla flavour in baking and desserts. Place a whole bean in a jar of sugar to make the vanilla sugar often called for in recipes; a bean can be used three or four times.

VINEGAR, RICE a colourless vinegar made from fermented rice and flavoured with sugar and salt. Also known as seasoned rice vinegar; sherry can be substituted.

WHEATEN CORNFLOUR see cornflour.

WONTON WRAPPERS and gow gee or spring roll pastry sheets, made of flour, egg and water, are found in the refrigerated or freezer section of Asian food shops and many supermarkets. These come in different thicknesses and shapes. Thin wrappers work best in soups, while the thicker ones are best for frying; and the choice of round or square, small or large is dependent on the recipe.

YAKI NORI see nori.

CONVERSION CHART

MEASURES

One Australian metric measuring cup holds approximately 250ml, one Australian metric tablespoon holds 20ml, one Australian metric teaspoon holds 5ml.

The difference between one country's measuring cups and another's is within a 2- or 3-teaspoon variance, and will not affect your cooking results. North America, New Zealand and the United Kingdom use a 15ml tablespoon. All cup and spoon measurements are level. The most accurate way of measuring dry ingredients is to weigh them. When measuring liquids, use a clear glass or plastic jug with metric markings.

We use large eggs with an average weight of 60g.

DRY MEASURES

METRIC	IMPERIAL
15g	½oz
30g	1oz
60g	2oz
90g	3oz
125g	4oz (¼lb)
155g	5oz
185g	6oz
220g	7oz
250g	8oz (½lb)
280g	9oz
315g	10oz
345g	11oz
375g	12oz (¾lb)
410g	13oz
440g	14oz
470g	15oz
500g	16oz (1lb)
750g	24oz (1½lb)
1kg	32oz (2lb)

LIQUID MEASURES

METRIC	IMPERIAL
30ml	1 fluid oz
60ml	2 fluid oz
100ml	3 fluid oz
125ml	4 fluid oz
150ml	5 fluid oz
190ml	6 fluid oz
250ml	8 fluid oz
300ml	10 fluid oz
500ml	16 fluid oz
600ml	20 fluid oz
1000ml (1 litre)	1¾ pints

LENGTH MEASURES

METRIC	IMPERIAL
3mm	⅛in
6mm	¼in
1cm	½in
2cm	¾in
2.5cm	1in
5cm	2in
6cm	2½in
8cm	3in
10cm	4in
13cm	5in
15cm	6in
18cm	7in
20cm	8in
23cm	9in
25cm	10in
28cm	11in
30cm	12in (1ft)

OVEN TEMPERATURES

These oven temperatures are only a guide for conventional ovens.
For fan-forced ovens, check the manufacturer's manual.

	°C (CELSIUS)	°F (FAHRENHEIT)
Very slow	120	250
Slow	150	275-300
Moderately slow	160	325
Moderate	180	350-375
Moderately hot	200	400
Hot	220	425-450
Very hot	240	475

The imperial measurements used in these recipes are approximate only. Measurements for cake pans are approximate only. Using same-shaped cake pans of a similar size should not affect the outcome of your baking. We measure the inside top of the cake pan to determine sizes.